Spiritual Doodle

Draw Out the Joy of Spiritual Growth

Myra Möyrylä

BALBOA.
PRESS

A DIVISION OF HAY HOUSE

Balboa Press books may be ordered through booksellers or by contacting:

Balboa Press
A Division of Hay House
1663 Liberty Drive
Bloomington, IN 47403
www.balboapress.com
1 (877) 407-4847

Print information available on the last page.

ISBN: 978-1-9822-2412-7 (sc)
ISBN: 978-1-9822-2414-1 (hc)
ISBN: 978-1-9822-2413-4 (e)

Library of Congress Control Number: 2019903445

Balboa Press rev. date: 03/27/2019

ACKNOWLEDGEMENTS

My whole goal in writing this book of patterns is to encourage people to expand their conscious awareness of the way life is proceeding and empower choices in that proceeding to create a life filled with wisdom, forgiveness, grace, dignity, and power, but lastly, to be willing to take risks for one's happiness within the spiritual power principle of win-win-win, which is explained later. I would first like to acknowledge all the beautiful and powerful clients of my Free Spirit Health & Wellness business, who created in me a sincere desire to sketch out how these patterns work. You all have been the reason I incidentally started a collection of patterns in sketch form, so thank you!

Next, I would like to thank Tim Michaelson for sitting with me in verbal rapport to make all these patterns teachable. He served as my first student and helped me refine how to explain these patterns. These patterns will continue to have their own evolution over each discussion in the future as well. His easy-going manner and laughter has made the intensity of this project enjoyable and possible. I hope to continue to collaborate into the future, as collaboration is not what comes easy to me, and I knew this book would be a test of my willingness to grow. Tim, you have made my collaboration attempt rewarding and I continue to find courage to grow this skill because of our work together.

My collaboration skills have also been strengthened by my editor, Margaret Helminen, who showed me how fun it can be to do the tedious work if you're in the right company.

She embraced my eclectic and dyslexic ways and worked hard to make this writing as understandable as I would allow her, and still let it sound like my voice as I read it. I have deeply appreciated the unconditional love and support that she has shared with me. It makes me truly believe there is no reason to feel like I'm going it alone in this world. Margaret, thanks so much for your attention to this book and the friendship while working together, truly such a joy.

I also thank The Hay House Writers Workshop I attended in Chicago which started to make the finished product feel more concrete for me and it was there I was introduced to Balboa Press. Without the phone calls from Balboa Press, and their friendliness of checking in, I may not have gotten this far.

Lastly, special thanks to my husband and son, and all my friends, family, and spirit family, for all their love and support while working on this project, and all the other eclectic business I attend to, while I live a dynamic joyful life of taking risks for my happiness. Life is magical when we all grow together in our own authentic, honest, powerful, joy-filled way. Love you all.

Preface

There are a countless number of self-help books in the market at this time. My book is unique in that it bridges the mental ability that forms reality—to the spiritual vision to see underneath reality—and create order in the ball of chaos inherent in a complex and challenging time in a person's life.

This ability to draw simple sketches to open a porthole of order and see it unfolding in patterns helps awareness and self-empowerment to grow. Growth and empowerment through spiritual awareness creates a self-governing adult that continues spiritual growth through a lifetime.

Spiritual growth is the exponential ability to come from unconditional love and compassion under deeper and deeper life pressures as we grow. It allows a person to respond in peace and choice, and create the possibility for the best potential outcome in even complex situations.

I believe Spiritual Doodle is a timely tool because there is a growing wave of counselors, therapists, psychologists, and social workers who are now opening up to bridging the gap between psychological function and spiritual growth. These people are thirsting for simple tools to help their clients and this is one of those tools. I have met and talked to some of these pioneering people at the Energy Psychology Conference. Energy Psychology is now accepted as continuing education for license renewal in psychology related fields.

I have field tested this tool for years on a large variety of clients. I have worked with people that are religious in various ways and it doesn't interfere with their structured belief systems. I have also worked with people who are spiritual but not religious.

It is enlightening and empowering for people across the differentials of knowledge, education, belief systems, and lifestyle. Spiritual Doodle invites deeper understanding but does not force nor evangelize any certain way of having to be in this world. Our only goal should be growth through experience for a lifetime.

People who aren't ready to acknowledge the spiritual aspects of their lives do well with these patterns because they come from nature and physics and there is no need to be tied to the spiritual aspect when mapping for this population. They can still grow and evolve from this information.

I believe we need to be supported at this time to move into greater awareness of our personal power and our ability to become conscious beings that share openheartedly and grow and evolve from all of life toward love, compassion and collaboration with each other.

Many books have bits and pieces of this information expressed in various ways. Many authors have spent time writing the science behind some of my patterns. I feel like my book delivers a simple tool to the facilitator or self-facilitator to get started in growing conscious awareness and how best to proceed while in a complex and challenging aspect of life.

Contents

Beginning Thoughts

These spiritual doodles have inspired many people to find their inner courage to move through a challenging complex time. The reciprocal value in watching faces start to shine with hope and courage is what has made me happy to share these doodles and collect more as the need arises. The doodles all started out of this desire to show people how my brain sees things in pictures and patterns, and evolved into a repeatable experience that I have now shared for years with people. My desire with this book is to share simple doodling for self-facilitation and for therapists to share them with clients.

My goal is to help return people to their powerful, authentic, joyful life that benefits themselves and others.

I am also a dreamer of world peace. I believe it is the inside out model of self-governing from the heart, through love, compassion, and collaboration that will recreate this world into the place our preciousness desires to inhabit.

To just do our small part with the feeling that there is nothing but time, paradoxically, even when we know we are here for a short time, is living life to its fullest potential and adding to the greater whole for a future expression of peace and joy.

SPIRITUAL DOODLE

Draw Out the Joy
of Spiritual Growth

I'm a self-diagnosed, eccentric, eclectic, dyslexic. Thank goodness for spell check because I have trouble spelling all the categories I find myself in. My gift in all these words though, is I see life in a very gestalt, right brained, *patterns and pictures* sort of way.

The downside is—I can come across scattered and absent minded about minor things, like finding my car keys or shoes while hurrying out the door, because I use magical thinking about time.

That aside, I listen to people as I work with the mind-body-spirit connection, and see underneath what they are saying as they discuss a complex or challenging aspect of their life. Finding a way to quickly sketch out what I see to open a porthole to spiritual growth potential in their current situation, has been borne out of deep desire to create powerful, free-spirited people who share their passions and gifts, first because it serves themselves, then others, then the greater whole for good. My goal is to help create healthy, powerful people who allow the world to be their neighborhood, and contribute in a personal way to the potential for world peace.

Spiritual Doodle maps out the invitation to grow through personal challenges and complexities. The patterns seem to emerge loosely rooted in nature, math, biology or physics.

It dawned on me, over time, that it would make sense when spirituality emanates from the same creative universal source as these disciplines. I'm willing to say nature shouts in fractals all the spiritual truths without a voice to evangelize, judge or hurry. Nature models the truths.

All my doodle patterns can be used individually or in concert with each other. I often draw out just one pattern to illustrate a simple concept. I sometimes spend a whole hour drawing a porthole of understanding for someone who feels highly charged around their current challenge. It is a joy to watch curiosity and inner courage start to emerge as understanding of the deep growth potential registers, and the frustration and overwhelm diminish. I have drawn these patterns on backs of envelopes, on scraps of paper while visiting with friends, and most often on yellow lined paper in session. I mainly use doodles as a pre-therapy tool to take some overwhelm and over-focus away from the body system, or during session to show one concept to bring greater awareness, intent and choice.

I once doodled out the patterns for a complete stranger during a conference I was attending. We kept crossing paths and I could see she was a beautiful, sparkling individual with a pattern that was visibly playing out in rapid succession right before my eyes. I again crossed her path in the courtyard. I offered to doodle for her and create a porthole into what was happening because she was clearly distressed. I demonstrated through doodling that she didn't understand her own spiritual equal value to others, and she was being impinged on by people who were unable to establish healthy rapport. I will never know her name, but she was shining with excitement when I drew patterns for her and she filled in the personal information that made sense to her. She quickly put it all together and realized where the pattern started that was repeating before us during the day. As we continued to cross paths she would share small ways that she saw her pattern was already collapsing with a reciprocal, healthy pattern emerging. A new inner courage and excitement had taken the place of distress in this lovely woman in a very short time. I could feel her new sense of power. What a joy to share such a simple tool to rekindle curiosity and growth.

I find three main themes in myself, my friends and clients at this time in the mind-body-spirit integration process. The first theme is to **relearn to embody our preciousness,** or innate value. The innate value is bound to the moment of showing up here as a spiritual system in a physical body to participate in this lifetime. We desire to own our preciousness and care for it gently.

The disconnection from preciousness or innate value can happen by believing value is earned by status in family, occupation, culture and community. Earned status can make value feel fragile and easily damaged or shattered, and need vigilance and work to maintain a feeling of worthiness.

Embodying preciousness invites openhearted vulnerability when negotiating relationships. We are hard wired to desire interconnection with each other, to truly be seen, heard and understood. Being agreed with is optional as long as respect is mutual. It is through relationships that growth occurs emotionally and spiritually.

The second theme is *our search for internal power.* Healthy power is noble and willing to come from peace, love and compassion. It understands that everyone is of equal value, including ourselves. This power is embodied internally and reflected externally as self-governing with the desire to create a healthy outcome. I call this the *inside out model of power.*

External power, which I refer to as the top down model, is often displayed in different levels of intensity in governments, religions, corporations, educational institutions, and even family systems. The top down power model creates order and compliance through desire for status, as well as fear of failure, shame, incarceration, shunning, expulsion, disfellowship, abandonment and hell.

We desire the power to control the possibility for success in our lives. However, we struggle with the very word, power, because we fear the consequences of the top down model as listed above and need re-education around power's two different broadcasts. Power from the top down model driven by fear and a desire for status, and the inside out model driven by internal peace and a desire for emotional freedom, are worlds apart in what is driving a desired outcome.

We can contribute best when our internal power to make decisions and take action is based on our own innate value, and respect of the innate value of others.

The third theme is *our search for enlightenment.* We are becoming free to ask, "Who am I and why am I here? Why do I do what I do? How am I to be happy in this chaos and complexity called life on earth? If I'm here to just survive, what is it worth? What more is possible for me and humanity as a whole? How can thriving be a possibility for me and my family?"

Asking these questions creates the intention to excavate the deeper aspects of life, and to choose to grow and evolve spiritually. Joy in life is growth and development throughout a whole lifetime coupled with the inner courage to take risk for happiness based on that growth. Until we reconcile taking risk for happiness, we spend energy avoiding risk, and seek survival and security as our goal. We have the capacity to emerge from the security template of life into the thriving template.

Spiritual Doodle can map out how to use awareness to create reconnection to preciousness, power, and enlightenment to catalyze deeper integration in body, mind and spirit. Empowered whole beings naturally desire to live in peace, joy, and harmony with self, others and their environment which I define as thriving. Empowered whole living is openhearted and vulnerable, and able to form deep intimate connections, sharing love and compassion openly while growing and evolving for a lifetime.

CHAPTER 1

THREE STRAND BRAID

Time, Destiny & Free Will

Pattern use: to bring focus to what an individual has control over, which is choosing from free will instead of trying to control everything and feeling overwhelm from not being in control.

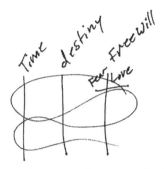

Time is linear to our human brain, which is the only concept of time necessary to explain this pattern. The brain records events in order, from first to last on a timeline, that can then be reviewed through memory. Time is an observable, but not controllable, element in life at this level of awareness, and needs to be factored this way to consciously move forward in life. We can see time but we can't control it. It starts marching with us as soon as we show up here, as a soul in a physical body.

Destiny is the concept of showing up purposefully at a time in history with a specific country, culture, gender and family to specialize who you are when you arrive in this lifetime.

Destiny is also considered within the concept of coming from, and being connected to, a divine intelligence. In the western religion the word God is used for this source. However, there are many names for the concept of the one intelligent source of love that connects and permeates all things.

The word Destiny has been used as a reason to explain why bad or good things happen to people. Within this reasoning, destiny isn't something that can be controlled, so we're left slapping out Destiny's fires the best we can, using patterns we inherited from those who influenced us most. I consider this explanation a *reflexive* response to Time and Destiny which is one way to learn from life—and there's no judgment, only learning potential.

Destiny, in my simple explanation, is something that arrives with us when we are born. As we start our movement through time we have only potentials of future possible outcomes. The moment of choice is in the present time, and then the outcome of choice is recorded as linear history. The past appears linear and the future is always in potentials. As we make choices in the present, the potentials shift to match the resonance of our current state or life. The future is always shifting with choices we make based on our current emotional, physical, and spiritual interpretation of life. This is what gives us the possibility to examine life through Free Will. The moment of choice is where the power to come out of reflexive responding is, and then it's possible to start creatively responding through conscious awareness of Free Will. This creates a co-creative collaboration with Time and Destiny.

Free Will is sometimes a controversial concept. Humans have created some complex and painful moments in personal and global history and it can be hard to take responsibility for those events as an individual, or an interconnected, global family.

Free Will, however, is our greatest power to own and use consciously. It is where we have the power to draw out of Destiny the highest potential outcome from our moment of choice in the present.

I see Free Will as a binary system in its most titrated explanation. Binary means operating on the system of two choices, and in Free Will, the two choices are fear or love. People have different reactions when they're afraid or feel love. Some derivatives or expressions of fear are anger, greed, betrayal, hate, racism and aggression. Love has other interchangeable expressions as well, such as peace, compassion, patience, kindness, and charity along with any other word for love in action. The surface expression of this binary system can be vastly different, but can be titrated to whether it is an act of fear or an act of love.

The binary filter system of Free Will operates in alternating current, meaning a continuous switching between coming from fear and coming from love, at each moment of choice in the present. We have the spiritual potential to learn deep wisdom from choosing *either* fear or love. Learning and embodying wisdom can only happen when we take ownership of our choices, actions, and results as we function in Free Will, which takes emotional and spiritual maturity—especially when our results create an outcome with painful consequences. The spiritual law of humbleness is about being willing to learn from *either* way.

The wisdom we glean from experience can then catalyze the inner courage to come from love and peace as we make choices in each moment, to draw out our highest potential outcome.

To understand and accept Free Will we have to surrender, and accept the fact that life is a continuous learning environment with no static outcome of perfection possible or required. Universal perfection is the chaos and entanglement that makes all outcomes possible, and reconciles Free Will as the source of personal power. Eventually, growing and learning become our joy in life, and sometimes the hardest thing to accept is that we never come to a finish point. Our spiritual goal is the continuous growth within understanding the power to come from love and peace as a natural expression of the connection to the universal, divine source of love.

To be governed internally by the inside out model of *spiritual right action* is the highest form of power. It creates a place where the potential for me to win—you to win, and the whole situation to have outcomes that reflect the highest good for all, is expressed. This is the Spiritual Law of Win-Win-Win.

Using Free Will to come from fear is the opposite of win-win-win, which is, I win—you lose, as the goal, and the model of dominance and control, or the war model, is reflected in the results of turbulence, chaos and struggle, and holds in place the need for the top down model of governing.

To reconcile Free Will power is to be willing to take full responsibility for our choices, actions, and outcomes even when we catch ourselves reflexively responding with patterns, or choosing to respond from fear.

We have a divine right to learn from all of our life experiences, but shame and judgment can inhibit that right and block our way to gaining wisdom. The choice is between judgment and wisdom. If wisdom is the goal, it is discernment of our results that allow learning from positive or negative outcomes. Shame and judgment, the very strategies that have been engaged to keep humanity on the straight and narrow, and perhaps the willingness to be controlled by the top down model, have been the same strategies that have kept us from connecting to our internal power through Free Will and choice, coupled with willingness to take responsibility for our outcomes.

Our powerful, spiritual responsibility is to become the best reflection possible of peace and love while honoring Free Will and its inherent learning curve that teaches us, through our freedom, to come from either fear or love in each moment. To do this we have to become unconditional lovers and forgivers of ourselves, and others entangled with us, as we each embody this same learning. These are the *Spiritual Law of Equal Value* and *Spiritual Law of Unconditional*

Love and Forgiveness that are sketched out in various ways through religious and spiritual traditions.

Our self-responsibility is to stay focused on our conscious choices through Free Will while being invited to surrender to Time and Destiny. Time marches with us as something to observe, but not attempt to control, as we move forward at the point of choice. Our Destiny shifts its potentials in the future as our outcomes of choice crystallize into our history in a linear story of life experience.

Our power of Free Will is always in the present moment and it is always operating in the binary system of choosing between fear and love. We use the wisdom of the past and the potentials of the future, but the creation is in the present only through Free Will choosing. Let us choose the most loving, peaceful, joyful life possible from our current level of knowledge, experience and wisdom.

Taking responsibility for outcomes is the key to experiencing knowledge and wisdom, but it is the most demanding path of self-love because we are accountable to our internal, governing model of desiring peace for ourselves and our world. Discernment coupled with wisdom filtered through love and peace allows for the highest outcome potential in each moment.

This is the best I can map out the convoluted concept of Free Will and why it is necessary for our spiritual growth as we consciously choose to reflect on our connection to the universal source of love.

In *my* life story, once I was under enough heat and pressure, I was invited to wrestle with the concept of, "Where do I have control in my life?" I realized early on, some factors in my life seemed out of my control, but had the power to severely impact me. Along with those factors, I also had three major losses in my early adult life. As a freshman in college my father died suddenly in a work accident. Then before I was 30 years old, I lost two stillborn children two weeks shy of two years apart. It was the third blow which made me realize that my culturally programmed, stoic pattern of response was not going to work anymore. I was being forced to go deeper than just pretending I was tough enough to move through Time and Destiny like I was fine.

I was at a choice point between being willing or not willing to embrace life. That choice was the difference between the potential to begin growing and flourishing despite my story, or it was going to be the beginning of withdrawal from my life in whatever form that took. Until there is an intention to choose, we will default to "choice" being a reflexive response to life through patterns acquired since childhood. I believe the single most important word in the spiritual journey is intention. When I was at this choice point, I didn't have the perspective I have now, as I'm writing this. I just felt it deep in my grieving, shattered body and soul—that using the same pattern of the stoic, "press on regardless" pattern was inadequate to foster me through the reconstruction of who I was, now that those events had irrevocably occurred. The truth is, I didn't want to be here to feel this tidal wave of pain. At the same time, I felt a need to surrender to the miracle of being alive after surviving the crisis of an iatrogenic hospital stay leading to the C-section stillbirth of my daughter.

I had a near-death experience during the time I spent in my hospital crisis. I can only describe that experience—as my self being in muted, golden-yellow light where all was understood in a ball of information without words—words which felt encumbering and limited. My first thought in words on return was, "It's not as fragile as it seems." I was made aware that when we leave our bodies we return to "what is love," and that is all that ever was, and is. The universal intelligence is the energy of love, and we are a part of that universal intelligence as our spiritual expression. That awareness made it hard to be back in my body where I had to experience the shattering pain of betrayal and loss, along with the uncertain state of my physical health. I also was aware that I had to surrender to being "in body" as *for* me, not against me, if I was going to heal emotionally, spiritually and physically. I knew I had to choose to start my healing work at all levels of my being, a task that seemed enormous and with no certain outcome assured. To begin the healing process seemed to tally up to more energy than I had, but to choose not to begin felt like it would cost me my life. My intention became the question, "What more is possible?"

During this time I also had post-traumatic stress symptoms of nightmares and sweating episodes that would make me wake up at night—unable to find my verbal expression—until I could snap out of it enough to talk. Once I could talk I would only say to my husband, "I had that dream again." To describe my nightmares at the time was too complex for me emotionally. I had anxiety about going to sleep, and if I experienced a nightmare episode, I would have anxiety about falling back to sleep. I felt like I couldn't find relief from grief of loss, and/or overwhelm of my shattered state. Even sleep was risky.

My intention to examine, "What more was possible?" started with having to ask myself, "Since you didn't get to stay in the soft, gold-light with no apparent physical body, can it be OK to now notice you're not afraid of dying while still in body?" I spent a year working on truly surrendering to living in body along with the grief and pain that could only organically be resolved through active work and time. I also cared for my body with the intention to show myself that I *wanted* to live and be healthy, even when I couldn't feel it as my truth yet.

"What more is possible?" has lead me from the beginnings I just described to now—where I can finally—better verbalize the profound effect that a near-death experience and my physical, emotional, and spiritual recovery has had on me. I am in paradox of wishing it hadn't all happened that way and glad I learned what I did.

The heat and pressure of complex challenges are our invitations to go deeper and start co-creating with Time and

Destiny by having to choose to see what more is possible when our survival strategies of reflexive response are no longer adequate. The more pressures we have at one time, the less filters we hold in place. These are the times that we are invited to grow.

I consider this the *Spiritual Law of Perfect Timing*. The timing will always be imperfect, perhaps even devastating to the logic of our brain, but perfect to the Higher Self that is in sync with the universal source of love.

Grappling with the concept of *Time, Destiny* and *Free Will* can be worthy of a book unto itself.

Drawing the Pattern of
the Three Strand Braid

Time, Destiny & Free Will

The first line signifies Time

Time starts moving forward with us when we show up here in this lifetime. Time can be observed but not controlled. Time gives us a linear interpretation of life.

The second line signifies Destiny

With our arrival, certain aspects of Destiny are crystallized
when we show up in this lifetime. We arrive with a specific
gender at a certain time in history—to parents with habits
and status, a culture, a native language, and a community
in a certain country. As we move through time our future is
in potentials which are always shifting with each choice we
make in the present moment. Our history is linear with Time
because it is the story of our choices we make in the present
along with the results.

The third line signifies Free Will

Fear and love for a binary system is Free Will.

Here it is important to explain that the control we have in
life is through Free Will, the binary filter that allows choice
from fear or love. Learning can come from either if we

drop judgment and learn wisdom from results. Consciously choosing between love and fear *is* power to co-create with Destiny and Time. When we come from *spiritual right action* we choose to come from love and peace, and can co-create the highest potential outcome and collaborate with the concept of win-win-win. Coming from love is our goal as we evolve spiritually.

**The weaving line braids them all together
as our life story.**

We can have vastly different outcomes when we move through life challenges depending on how we choose to filter our experience through love or fear as we move forward with Time and Destiny.

CHAPTER 2

Parabola or Bell Curve

Positive, Negative, and Neutral Files

Pattern use: to bring perspective to an individual who is over focused on one aspect of their life and helps open their focus to see the value inherent in any aspect of their life.

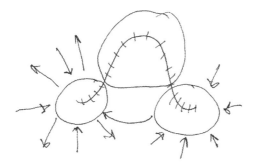

Human behavior is one of the most complex fields of study because everyone in some way is like a free radical out on their own—saying and doing what works for them in each moment. And yet in some ways, they are acting predictable— as seen in personality typing systems—where we love to find our type, and laugh and acknowledge which category summarizes us best.

We recognize ourselves in these brilliant systems of personality typing that can be anywhere from quite old to very modern. They help us understand ourselves and others in a composite way so it's possible for us to go about the business of learning how to work across the strata of different personalities and natures.

I'm self-taught in several personality typing methods to help understand myself, my husband, son, friends, and clients, and to aid in my communication with them.

I also use my knowledge of personality systems routinely in my work as a dental hygienist to quickly establish rapport, and instill a sense of safety for my patients.

This said, it still only scratches the surface of human variations and choices in both communication and action. So many things have to be factored in to understand each unique person, and personality is just a place to start. There is also age, gender, family systems, culture, lifestyle, physical health, mental health, diet, education, knowledge, experience, trauma, wisdom, financial status, community, religion, country, climate and more, that contribute to who we are and how we respond to life.

Underneath all of the variables just mentioned, the template of our positive, negative, and neutral files is likened to the bell curve. Remember, after a test in school, you waited to see where you fell in the bell curve?

It was exciting to set the curve or be on the end of the curve marking the highest grades, but quite dreadful to find yourself on the other end where the lowest grades were also fewer and just as highly charged, but in a negative way.

If you were in the largest portion of the bell, meaning somewhere in the middle of the pack with an average grade, there was a feeling of relief that you survived it somewhere in the neutral, non-dramatic middle of the pack.

In my life as a student I've hung out in all areas of the bell curve after a test. I know that nobody liked the person who set the curve with the highest grade, and the person with the lowest grade is working on liking themselves after a test like that, at least that is my memory of both ends.

Coming out of the classroom memories and into the Spiritual Doodle meaning of the bell curve drawing, I will first explain how I use the word *files*. Like a computer, we all have multiple files stored in us. We can pull them up on the front screen for review and use at any time.

Within us we have files on how to be polite, kind, generous, knowledgeable, educated, wise, talented, gifted, productive, satisfied, joyful, loving, peaceful, and other files on the positive side of the bell curve that are on the same end as having the highest grade.

We also have our shadow files like being fearful, unkind, selfish, restless, impatient, mean, stressed, nervous, jealous, angry, prejudiced, dishonest, bereaved, sad, depressed, and others along those lines that we, if possible, would rather not show people or experience if we can help it. These are the files at the other end of the bell curve that bring us to the place likened to finding out you've received the lowest grade on the test.

Neutral files are all the files in the middle that make up the largest portion of the bell like the average test grades of the pack where most people are and nobody sticks out in any special way.

Neutral files are where we connect with our daily activities in a mundane way like standing in the grocery store line, putting gas in the car, brushing our teeth, tying our shoes, moving about the house to straighten things up, driving to the next destination, going through the day's work, play, or rest—when nothing is highly charged.

Slow down the day and imagine it frame by frame. A lot of time is actually spent in neutral files just going about activities without any high charge on them, the people, or the surrounding environment.

Neutral files serve the purpose of energy conservation so that life can be processed while moving forward. Similar to yoga and other work I have studied, the philosophy: learning and integration come in the stillness, holds true here as well. However, life is connected to time and movement. The mundane aspects of life are the stillness where integration and learning take place if that is the intention.

The sense of autopilot in an ordinary day allows time to process the learning that is mainly catalyzed by the two ends of the parabola, where the positive files and negative files challenge us in unique and charged ways, if the intention is to grow and develop.

Negative files serve to catalyze the struggle to grasp and understand innate value, preciousness, and worthiness of unconditional love, while observing the imperfections of the unique inner world and outer actions reflecting our fears, anger, stress or other shadow aspects inherently residing in the negative or dark files.

Positive files, which I also call gifts and talent files, are where grappling with being visible in an authentic and passionate lifestyle, both personal and professional, is the ultimate challenge. Surprisingly, this visibility can bring about a lot of fear, sometimes even holy terror, hence the statement, "We fear success more than failure."

When functioning from a place congruent with authenticity some will love us, some will not like us, and most will never know we exist—again the bell curve—and that has to be acceptable. It is not possible to function from a place where we always only receive approval and still be able to be honest and authentic.

The shadow files or dark files we have at the far end of the bell curve can be compared to the lowest grades on the test curve. They are the files creating the most grief, struggles, suppression, reluctance, and regrets in our life.

Author, Debbie Ford, in her book, *The Dark Side of Light Chasers* maps out the shadow side and how to reconcile it. I recommend this book if embracing your own shadow files seems obscure or complex.

These files need to be acknowledged in ourselves because they allow us the experience to receive love and compassion even when we are in a place that we have nothing to offer in return.

I have been in dark places of grief and betrayal with my hospital experience that led to my C-section and stillborn daughter. Along with healing from the crisis and surgery, I had post-traumatic stress symptoms that entangled me in dark frustration and I feared the symptoms would be never ending.

This dark file felt left on my screen for days at a time, and from here I gained understanding and compassion for people who choose to end their pain by ending their life. I felt a strong desire to not be here in my agony and grief.

I would feel slight pain relief when I fantasized about walking away or driving away until I died. I never believed I would act on these thoughts but I would use the fantasy to help me survive for one more moment.

I even used fantasizing about dying as motivation for getting out of bed, by promising myself that if I take a shower and get ready for work, then the act of driving to and from work would give me two chances of someone causing an accident with me that would let me out of here and out of my pain.

It is interesting to remember this dark place because it was real and overwhelming at the time. However, the only lingering effect is I no longer judge suicide. I get it.

I also understand how hard it was for people who cared about me to know how dark my world felt at that time. I remember protecting them from how long that dark place lasted by not showing I was still stuck there as best I could.

I grew awareness of how people in dark places need to be heard without judgment or fear from the listener. The most complex part of this for the listener is that danger does exist, and the listener doesn't have control over the Free Will and choice of the person suffering their current challenge.

The most therapeutic listening was when the listener would stay peaceful and loving but willingly heard me out and allowed me to be visible in my pain.

Unconditional love is about loving without needing a specific safe outcome to be assured. I felt alienated by people who feared my pain and wanted me to promise them I was OK.

I was very loved and supported by the people brave enough to sit with my pain and not be afraid nor pretend they could be the solution.

Besides my husband, I had a hygienist friend at the office where I worked, that could meet me in every moment of my grief. She had lost both her parents six months apart to separate health related deaths when she was a teenager. She knew what shattering grief was and how it felt.

She interviewed at my dental office the day I found out I was expecting my daughter. As we worked together she went through both my stillborn pregnancies and recoveries with me. Then she moved back to Iowa, her original home state.

She was my angel in the unaware. She could laugh with me if I found the strength to find humor in something, and she could give me comfort in a few words if she walked into my room and found me crying between patients. She simply met me in whatever file I was honestly in and loved me there.

I learned so much about unconditional love and support from her modeling it for me, and have always felt like she was sent with the *Law of Perfect Timing* to march with me through Time and Destiny for five, deeply challenging years.

She had been through grief and could understand what I needed. She modeled the learning she had done in her own shadow files of grief, and brought the knowledge into the gifts and talent files where she could shine understanding and share unconditional love with me.

In our dark files we have the capacity to learn to drop judgment and grow compassion first for ourselves, and then for others who are traversing their own dark files.

I understand more completely than before, that when you enter into grief, fear, hurt, anger, and betrayal, you have big decisions to make to either start a downward spiral of despair and destruction, or to find your courage to grow from the complex parts of life—a Free Will choice that nobody can make for you on your solitary, spiritual journey.

Even in that low place of grief and pain I was overwhelmed by the people who showed up when I had nothing to offer but my grief. Friends and family would share their time and love with me when I had absolutely nothing of value to reciprocate.

I realized that having nothing to offer was to also experience what unconditional love really felt like when being received. It felt both deeply humbling and deeply healing to experience the outpouring of concern and caring from people brave enough to be in my presence. I was touched by the cards that came in the mail and the calls of support.

I went back to work in the dental office a month after my first stillborn loss. Some patients, although virtual strangers to me, were vulnerable enough to share stories of similar grief and offer their sincere support. I remember feeling surprised and would have never guessed they had grieved like me because they looked so normal. I, at the time, felt like I looked shattered and broken and that it would always be visible in my body. I felt hope for myself as they shared openheartedly.

As people shared unconditional love and support, it reconnected me with my understanding that my value is innate and precious. I also came to realize that a lot of us, including myself, somehow think value is earned and easily diminished.

Part of the healing journey is to reinstate the awareness of innate value or preciousness that is not about function, but about being a soul in a physical body that is purposefully here. We are all purposefully here and of equal value, which again is the *Spiritual Law of Equal Value.* I like to say, "If you have breath and a pulse, that is your equal right to be here and take up space and breathe oxygen without apologizing for it." At this spiritual level it is impossible to be less or more valuable than anyone else.

The soul or spiritual aspect of being human is a fractal of the divine intelligence, and its value is tied to that intelligence whether in or out of body.

Being here is an invitation to simply learn about choosing love when we also have the contrast or possibility of choosing from fear while in body. Life is set up so that either choice can teach us something valuable about love and peace if it is our intention to learn.

In the positive end of the bell curve model—the gifts and talent files, the reflection of the learning, through receiving unconditional love while challenged in the shadow files, can be freely expressed without reciprocation necessary.

In the gifts and talent files, we can reflect unconditional love, learned when we experience negative files—about fear or how we feel betrayed or rejected. This is where we suffer. This is where people can reflect to us that we still have love that's available to us even when we have nothing to offer, so it's like the training. This is like our understanding of, "What does unconditional love really mean?" And we can take this learning over to the talent files and reflect love without asking anything in return.

My hygienist friend modeled her learning so beautifully, having preceded me in her learning from her teenage experience of deep grief.

Learning how to surrender to receive unconditional love while in dark places allows the learning to transfer to the positive, or gifts and talent files, and become a reflection of that learning by sharing unconditional love through actions and words. Now there is an understanding of how that love feels and why it has such value.

When love can be expressed in an openhearted, vulnerable way, it serves others and us equally. We are made to express love and peace as a natural part of who we are spiritually, and it either feels neutral or gives us energy when we share in this context.

When we bring unconditional love and peace to our work or occupation, (that which occupies our time) it then becomes our profession, our unique spot in the world where we profess unconditional love and peace, despite whatever title we may possess at work.

Professing love and peace is mostly done in a nonverbal way. It is regulated by our physiology being at peace, not pretending we are peaceful. Nonverbal communication, I have read, is 80% of our communication. If our physiological state, meaning our body chemistry, matches what we are saying, then what we say has value because it's congruent.

It is congruent to talk about being peaceful when our body is at peace as much as it is congruent to talk about being upset or worried when our body is in fight or flight reaction and not peaceful.

Congruency in our communication is a form of honesty. It's what keeps us feeling safe together, and builds trust. Congruency is what children look for in communication with adults to feel safe and secure in their world.

When we are in stress and we are pretending we are fine, the nonverbal communication is incongruent with the verbal, and we give away our power to the confusion we create. Congruency in communication is the body and our words matching our truth in the moment.

Honesty through congruency is power in communication because it creates an invitation to intimacy and openhearted communication.

Drawing the Pattern of the Bell Curve Parabola

Positive, Negative, and Neutral Files

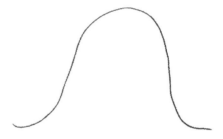

The bell curve line drawn out represents a full spectrum of files within a person—likened to a bell curve for test averages in a class.

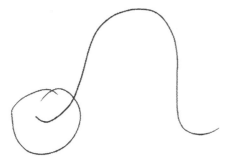

The positive files, or gifts and talent files, are on the left, and a circle is drawn around the approximation of the files that are the positive highlights of what's within a full spectrum person, likened to the highest grades in the bell curve for a test in a class.

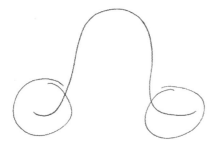

The negative files or shadow files, which sometimes are called dark files are on the right, and a circle is drawn around the approximation of the files that are the negative or shadow aspects of what's within a full spectrum person (we are all full spectrum) likened to the lowest grades in the bell curve for a test in a class.

The neutral files are the largest part of the bell curve or parabola, and a circle is drawn around the neutral files of the full spectrum person—like the abundant average grades in the class test parable.

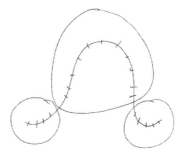

The hash marks are to show that the full spectrum has multiple files throughout the parabola.

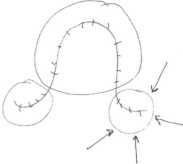

Arrows are drawn inward to the negative or shadow files circle to depict receiving unconditional love and support while in a place of having nothing to offer in reciprocation.

The possibility to learn about innate value and preciousness is catalyzed through the receiving of unconditional love.

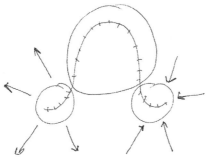

Arrows drawn outward in the positive or gifts and talent files circle show that what was learned is now being reflected through the giving of unconditional love and support through our words and actions.

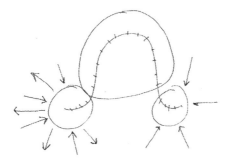

Arrows drawn inward in the positive or gifts and talent files circle depict being open to receiving love and support as well as appreciation, but with no contract or agenda to shore up personal value or necessity. The learning has been complete enough in the shadow files to know that our value is innate and our preciousness assured.

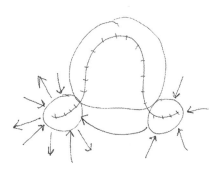

The arrow between the negative files, where the learning about unconditional love takes place, and the positive files, where the modeling of unconditional love through words and actions take place shows how necessary both ends of the bell curve are for spiritual growth.

CHAPTER 3

Fibonacci Spiral

Repeating Patterns

Pattern use: to bring awareness to the potential for growth and to form a new perspective when a life event is feeling highly overwhelming.

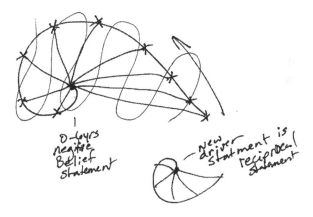

Self-responsibility is the key to this pattern. The goal here isn't to blame yourself, nor to blame someone else if you avoid self-responsibility. The goal is to co-create, through Free Will and conscious choice with Time and Destiny, in even the most complex circumstances, to draw out the highest potential outcome.

We are playing in the quantum field, where everything in the future is in potentials and continuously responding and fluidly shifting to our choices in the moment. The present moment is the only place we choose and the only place our body can serve us as a tool while here, in this life.

Our history, at least for the scope of this pattern, is linear and is a string of choices, experiences, and results that can be put in order from first to last.

We have two choices to respond to Time and Destiny that have been mentioned earlier. They are *reflexive responding* and *co-creating*. Most of us move between reflexive responding and co-creating in alternating current. The goal is to evolve throughout a lifetime so more and more time can be spent conscious enough to co-create.

Reflexive responders are people who have not reconciled Free Will and see life within the context of survival. Reflexive responders slap out the fires around them with the same strategies over and over, which only intensifies the belief that life is a struggle and it's never safe. These strategies are mostly formed in childhood.

Bruce Lipton, Ph.D., says in his book, *The Biology of Belief,* "the fundamental behavior, beliefs and attitudes we observe in our parents become hard-wired as synaptic pathways in our subconscious minds. They control our biology for the rest of our lives…unless we can figure out a way to reprogram them." Dr. Lipton also states that this subconscious brain state is between birth and six years old.

By the time we are adults we are often using strategies that came on board during childhood, and stem from beliefs that we can not consciously recall. We only see the results of our adult actions that can fall short of our desired goals. This can be very obvious in our communications when we feel misunderstood, accused, marginalized, disliked or all other signs that our connection with another person or group of people is not proceeding as desired.

Co-creators live in awareness and choice and are willing to learn from everything. There has to be a willingness to be *curious* with any result that is brought on by free choice, and to glean the wisdom instead of halting the learning possible with judgment.

"Oh interesting, I wonder what I'm learning?" instead of, "Oh no, how could this happen to me?" is the shift in awareness that opens the door for learning. That being said, it is imperative to process any pain or grief because spiritual bypass or denial will not allow us to grow compassion for ourselves and others.

It is possible to recycle any experience into wisdom if we abstain from judgment and stay curious and humble.

If sharing compassion and unconditional love is the goal of wisdom, we can only understand it by receiving and giving it in reciprocal rapport **with ourselves** and others. The rich matrix of opportunity for learning love and compassion is always presented as movement through life happens.

Now that we have an understanding of self-responsibility we can go back to the Fibonacci Spiral doodle for repeating patterns. Patterns playing out in our lives function in either a positive or a negative way.

Our goal is to never think we can function outside of patterns, but to spot the negative patterns and collapse them, and put into place a positive reciprocal pattern that supports growth and development of life.

The pattern starts with a seed point that comes into our life as a newly acquired belief. In the case of the negative patterns it would be a negative or destructive belief. As we mentioned earlier in this book, beliefs are often coming from childhood, when interpretation was filed like a fact at a young age, and now isn't consciously recalled. I call this seed point the driver of the pattern.

After the seed point, time starts to move forward but curls around this point, as repeating patterns of the driver start to occur. The driver can be unknown but the results are observable in a sequence that is repeating with some variables.

Each time an event repeats, it points back to the driver and is interpreted one of two ways; one interpretation is the intensification of the belief which is often interpreted as reality. The other interpretation sees it as an invitation to spot the pattern driving from a seed point as it repeats itself.

Our intention is to see the present moment challenge as being a part of a pattern and then discover what the driver is even if the seed point isn't remembered.

The clues are in the way it repeats. Trusting that the pattern is there helps locate how it is repeating, and finding the belief that drives it, even if the seed point is not conscious.

Once we see the pattern for what it is, collapse of the pattern begins. It only holds in place as reality when it is driving underneath the ability to spot it. As the pattern collapses with the negative driver then we consciously start the reciprocal pattern with the positive or healthy driver that will be left in place.

Again, everything functions in patterns and it is impossible to leave a void. The reciprocal pattern is just its opposite aspect of the old pattern, like the heads side of the coin instead of tails.

In my own life, the most important pattern that I was finally able to spot was driving from the belief, "A woman with power over me will get what she needs from me while my needs are subservient or ignored." This pattern was driving out loud and big before I spotted it and was able to collapse it.

My pattern actually started out previous to *my* life in the generational trickle-down effect of unresolved matriarchal imbalance.

My mother had this same pattern that repeated from her own C-section birth after three days of labor to save her mother. My mother was born with the cord wrapped around her neck three times. My grandmother also had schizophrenia during a time when not much could be done and quite a bit of superstition still surrounded mental illness.

During her life up until four years-old my mom lived in fear of her mentally ill mother and had to worry about the two sisters that were younger than her as well.

She remembers hiding with those two babies under her bed while her mother ranted about the devil. There went my mom's feeling of safety and comfort from her matriarch.

At four years-old my mom experienced the loss of her mother completely when she was institutionalized for schizophrenia in a facility four hours away from home. Now she had to experience loss and be parented by a father and five older brothers while she continued to feel protective of her two younger sisters.

I was born to my mom when she was twenty. I was her second child and her first daughter. My role with my mother, incidentally, became a mothering role to her. I used to laugh as a teenager and joke, "I'm my mother's mother."

I now know that the role I took on put a dent in my childhood development and left the seed point of the unconscious belief that would continue to drive out in my life.

Since it wasn't on my front screen all the time during my childhood years, I couldn't see it as having any deep role in my life. I had never lived without the pattern either, so it was just my reality.

Like any young person, I enjoyed many learning opportunities such as violin and piano lessons, girl scouts, 4H, orchestra, band, choir, cross country and swimming. I looked like I had it all at a glance, including good grades and a warrior spirit to say with determination, "I always get what I want."

My college years looked much the same, other then the moment my dad died. A college friend told me, twenty-five years later, "The uncanny part of our friendship is that I saw how big it was for you when your dad died, and when you got back from the funeral I never saw or heard anything about it again." My response, after the funeral, was rooted in my stoic culture where you don't cry and you don't talk about it.

Meanwhile, I was almost a straight A student, and at all the honor convocations, however, my goals were fueled by sheer terror of failure, also known as perfectionism. Only my college roommate witnessed how scattered I was.

I also enjoyed playing my saxophone in three college bands and enjoyed intramural broomball and one year of varsity swim team. I looked like an all American college student.

My dark files were never reflected back to me as significant because I did my best to keep them hidden. I had a deep feeling of going it alone while surrounded by good friends that I just wasn't willing to be vulnerable with to get support.

This all hid well the frantic feeling of walking into my first day of dental hygiene school during my second year of college, and having it dawn on me that for the next two years I would be submerged in women only. I was already lacking support from my family. My mom, in her grief over the death of my father, was in chaos, and my dad was gone.

Now I felt the fear of women in power over me sink in, once I sat down in the back of the class, with my shoulder against the wall. I saw pieces of this pattern, but I never saw it as a pattern. It was driving from my sense of reality and I was in survival mode using perfectionism to reach my goals.

The level of intensity in the curriculum and the speed at which it had to be learned was nothing short of academic boot camp, but I had the extra stress of my pattern.

On my first day in clinic, my instructor asked me if I was the one on the swim team. I thought she was excited for me, because it was the first year that my college had a girl's swim team. Instead, she looked at my enthusiastic nineteen-year-old face and said, "When I saw your name on the list, I thought to myself, you'll never make it." She turned and left and my heart sank. She was the instructor who would spend the next ten weeks giving visual assessments of my clinic work and she had already failed me.

My pattern spoke in similar ways sprinkled throughout my remaining college career, and none of the instructors who played into my pattern apologized for their comments when I graduated at the top of that year's class.

The pattern that is obvious now, was a painful reality back then that kept me in survival and perfectionism.

I also had female instructors that supported me and reflected their belief in me, but they didn't match my pattern so I couldn't resonate with the support they offered, nor did I trust it.

In patterns, there are usually choices of what to focus on. Focus is given to what matches the belief, even when the belief is hidden.

After I graduated I started working back in my home town. I was hired quickly by my childhood dentist, who was a man, so all was well.

His assistant of many years resented me and she played into my pattern beautifully by scheduling patients into my lunch, even when I wouldn't get paid for it and just showed me quietly I was not being supported by her. We were able to confront and resolve that conflict, and lots of time went by fairly smoothly there.

My first pregnancy, which I mentioned earlier, was another repeating pattern of women in power over me. The doctor and I could have avoided this moment that we created together if I had just grown enough to trust my own intuition, and if I had already collapsed the pattern. Surprisingly, this is not where I could spot it yet as a pattern.

Then during my second pregnancy that also ended in stillbirth, an associate dentist, again a woman, started to work at my office.

With my pattern in place, our relationship was turbulent right from the start. Although she was younger than me, she was a dentist and I was a hygienist, a differential in status and power.

Slowly our working relationship eroded until I was back driving perfectionism, similar to my college strategy for survival.

She shared enough of her personal story with me to see that we were similar, but I still couldn't see *my* pattern driving until my health was deteriorating with irritable bowel syndrome and weight loss as well as a complete stop to my menstrual cycle. I was emaciated with muscle loss and I could feel myself almost spontaneously passing out from everything being metabolically and physiologically imbalanced. I still could not see how my interpretation of this complex relationship was creating my reality and health imbalance.

I kept hoping all my symptoms stemmed from the grief of losing yet another stillborn child, this time a son. I didn't want to give up my job, which was the only constant in all the loss in my personal life.

Finally, I was walking through my kitchen and I had the statement crash through my denial in my head, "If you stay you will die." I stopped moving and waited for more information, but nothing more downloaded into my mind, but I knew instantly that I was being forced to leave my job to heal my body and spirit, emotionally and physically.

It dawned on me at this time why people choose to stay in overly complicated relationships. I was convinced that someday commonsense would rule the day and we could work peacefully together if I just tried harder to be more perfect and tried to explain to her what I thought was not working.

I wouldn't look at any other solution, because I didn't want to leave my work. The boss we had at the time was not a man who liked to confront conflict, so nothing resolved through his leadership either.

I finally fired myself, and left a letter of resignation on his desk. I removed my personal belongings from the office, dropped my keys through the mail slot, and walked away. My cycle switched back on and started two days after I had told my boss my truth about how things were going for my work partner and I. My irritable bowel syndrome stopped in two weeks when I walked away *after* two and a half years of misery.

It took two years to reclaim my health, but the biggest gain from that experience was that I finally saw my pattern that I had of women in power over me.

Once a pattern is spotted it cannot remain hidden and driving. I have paid the highest price for the wisdom gained in this pattern. I now insist I am willing to listen to whispers of intuition and that I don't have to be such a tough nut to crack that the pattern has to shout from the rooftops before I can see it.

Once I recognized that pattern and collapsed it, the evidence of its collapse came when I realized that all the places I had carefully set up to have men in charge flipped into being women.

In the local bank my favorite banker was a man, but when we called to take out our next loan only a woman was available. She became a great help and answered all our questions and got us what we needed in a timely and friendly no-nonsense way that I have always appreciated from her.

She would meet with me spontaneously if I stopped by with a question while we were in the process of looking at several different apartments to purchase and I needed information. It was a total joy to work with this powerful woman who is now happily retired, and I see her in the community as the same dynamic person.

The dentist I worked for was a fabulous woman. She allowed me to work the schedule of my choosing, so I could take time to travel and play, and pursue my other interests. She supported me and there was room for us to both be smart, dynamic women who desired to serve our patients.

My husband and I also worked with the owner of a travel agency, another powerful woman in our community, when we traveled to visit our families in Finland. She was also Finnish and had already been there. She took interest in making sure our dreams came true when we traveled the first time with elderly relatives. The second trip was a three month adventure that she choreographed. She shared our enthusiasm for adventure and said she'll vicariously enjoy the trip through us. We went to hike, kayak, and backpack, as well as spend plenty of time laughing and talking with relatives.

She has become my quiet, powerful mentor and we try to meet once a year to catch up. In retirement from the travel agency, she now sells real-estate and patiently showed us more than one property while we created rental income. Well past retirement age, she is energetic and well worth emulating in her enthusiasm for life.

I also have created a peaceful place to allow my mom to be who she is in our personal relationship. I honor her for going to college after my dad died, while raising seven kids, and graduating as a nurse. She has her own powerful way and has survived all her adversity.

The pattern is collapsed and I am free to enjoy a more dynamic, full spectrum connection to women in power over me, and in general. The reciprocal pattern in the old pattern's place is driving from the belief that women in power over me support me and ask nothing from me, and sharing time is without contract.

It took five years after spotting the woman pattern to see the quieter, less complex pattern I played out with men. My dad always seemed like the more emotionally stable person, albeit, it was probably mostly his stoic nature. He also was predictable in his actions, even when I didn't agree with him. I grew up wanting to emulate my dad more then my mom and I felt like he quietly believed in me and liked my warrior spunk. My secondary pattern was—I need men to shore me up while women are unpredictable and not for me.

Once I was able to see that pattern, I could see how I always felt safer having male teachers in elementary school and high school. I seemed to luck out and get the good teachers.

Then when I would get the woman teachers my experience was just the opposite, except for kindergarten and third grade. Those two teachers were fabulous women but I didn't know how to receive their support. I just felt a little safer.

In my first year of college I was in pre-science. I had a male professor who was my advisor and anatomy professor. He took me aside during the second term and asked me why I don't just pack up and go to dental school. He offered to help me set up the paper work to transfer. He said I would learn that I am smarter than the dentist and it will bother me, so I might as well go now. It was very flattering, but I didn't want to be that far into college loans by the time I was done. My parents were in financial despair, and that was only about to get worse when my father died later that term, so I understood I couldn't ask for any help from home. He then offered to let me teach his anatomy lab, which again was flattering, but I was involved with so many other activities I didn't think I would be able to fit it in.

He was encouraging me to find a higher educational path because he believed in me, just like my dad always stoically did. I continued to discuss things with him during my next two years even though I had an advisor from the hygiene program. I felt like I could trust his opinion on certain things more easily.

The hygiene advisor I had was a woman in total support of all my activities, and she worked hard to arrange my schedule to suit my needs; but again, I wasn't ready to receive support that well from her because of my pattern being strongly in place.

We have since rekindled our acquaintance at the hygiene conferences I attend for my continuing education. It is so fun to finally receive her support openheartedly and learn more of her story as well.

Four years after collapsing my pattern with women, my pattern with men became apparent to me although at first glance it seemed a positive thing. I realized I needed a male to shore me up while I had these imbalanced females around me.

With this male pattern driving out almost unnoticed, my childhood dentist, who became my first boss, always quietly believed in me. I shone under the trust he placed in me to meet my patients' needs, and I understood his way of setting up treatment plans for their care. I would have everything charted for him by the time he came in. I always felt like my intelligence was appreciated.

I realized the pattern with men which actually came to me in a dream, and I woke up teary and with full awareness. I could see immediately why it was so hard to leave the complex relationship with the associate dentist; it was because I would have to give up who I had unconsciously surrogated for my dad, who died when I was 19. I started working for this male dentist when I was 21. I realized that was my violation to him because it was a contract that wasn't appropriate—I was creating a connection that was fear based—and understood why I was so confused when he wouldn't stand up for me in that office conflict. It became clear, and started the collapse of men having to shore me up, while women were volatile and unpredictable.

A contract is the opposite of unconditional love because unconditional love asks nothing, and then more becomes possible in intimate rapport. Conditional love is a contract and people can be offended. We have to show up guarded, because we feel fragile; and conditional love is based on need even if the need is subtle.

Now I can feel the freedom to enjoy friendship and connection with both men and women. The patterns are no longer interfering with negotiating a relationship that is openhearted and honest.

This pattern, although not as costly to my health, still stunted my emotional freedom to respond to life in the present moment with healthy patterns. The pattern of needing men to shore me up is now replaced with the reciprocal pattern of: I take care of myself and enjoy healthy friendship with men and women.

The Fibonacci Spiral of repeating patterns is helpful when trying to shed light on a complex challenge that is creating turbulence and seems like a large, dark ball of chaos. To roll out the pattern and locate the driver is liberating to the emotional life, and growth producing for spiritual awareness.

Next, the reciprocal pattern driver is developed consciously. Intention to see both the original pattern and its driver collapsing, and the reciprocal pattern and its healthy belief start driving, is what assists the transition to the healthy pattern, as the old pattern fades away until gone. The willingness to ride out the remaining pattern that is shouting loud as it fades is necessary. Intention, when working with this pattern is everything.

Drawing the Fibonacci Spiral

Repeating Patterns

The dot in the center signifies the seed point of the pattern and usually comes on board as a belief between ages 0 to 6. This will become the point where the belief starts driving the pattern forward in time.

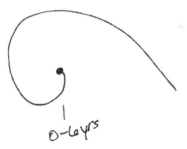

From there the line drawn out in a spiral is time moving forward but curling around the seed point of the pattern.

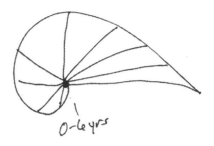

0-6 yrs

Then the connecting lines from the spiral to the seed point show repeating patterns of the belief from its seed point.

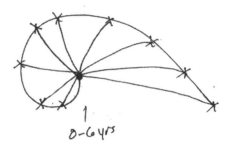

0-6 yrs

An 'x' on each of the lines shows that each of these repeating patterns can intensify the belief and feel like reality, or it can be seen as an invitation to see it as a pattern.

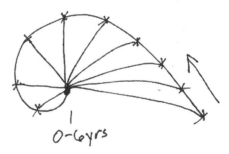

0-6yrs

The arrow pointing back is when the pattern is spotted and the driver of the pattern can now be discovered even if the seed point cannot be consciously remembered. Often something significant can be remembered and that is a good clue, and I will call it the seed point.

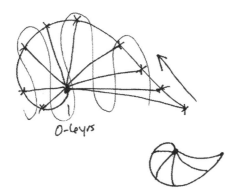

O-6yrs

Then the reciprocal pattern is drawn just starting next to the collapsing pattern. It will be small and a whisper, and the loud, old pattern may have to be ridden out while it fades, but the intent is on the new pattern—so draw a wavy line through the large, fading pattern.

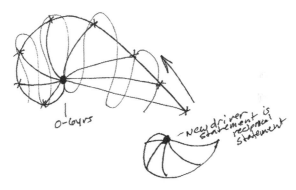

O-6yrs

New driver is reciprocal statement

Find the reciprocal driver and let that be the positive driver of the pattern that will support you for the rest of your life. Remember, everything is functioning in patterns, some just have negative consequences and others are healthy and positive.

CHAPTER 4

Atom Model of Intimate Rapport

Pattern use: to understand that communication between people can always be open hearted but at different levels of depth, that way we can let down our guard and enjoy connection with people.

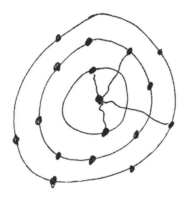

In this chapter I will discuss the concept of intimate rapport, which is based on authentic communication at different levels of intimacy.

This is an important concept to map out because people are searching for authenticity and honesty. However, many people only feel safe when masking themselves from others to protect their preciousness from judgment, criticism, rejection or other forms of not being accepted for who they naturally are in each moment.

It can be a relief to find out that authenticity is not an all or nothing principle of either someone knows everything about you, like a foot all the way on the gas pedal, or nothing authentic about you like a foot all the way on the brake pedal.

We all have the right to be authentic and many have the desire to be showing up honestly, but we negotiate with each other about how much personal information feels safe to share.

It takes time to build trust to go deeper into intimate rapport. Healthy rapport is negotiated between people at an honest level of safety and trust.

I feel all rapport is an intimate exchange when we are authentic in our presentation both non-verbally and verbal.

For example, if I am standing in the grocery store line I am still being authentic whether I speak to anyone or not. I may just be standing there, but people who are in non-verbal rapport with me will still see me and know perhaps my gender, approximate age, height, fashion style, and a few more things that are easily visible. That is still me being authentic and in rapport, just at a superficial level of intimacy.

If I smile and start a conversation and we find out we have the same type of work or same age children and choose to spontaneously deepen our rapport just a step before we are both on our way, although still superficial it helped us enjoy our time stuck in line by sharing honestly. In honest sharing we feel visible and connected to humanity. In short, we feel more loved.

The atom in Chemistry or Physics as our Spiritual Doodle for intimate rapport is perfect because it has a nucleus and electron rings. If intimate rapport models after the atom, then the nucleus represents a person and the electron rings represent different levels of intimate rapport for that person. The electrons represent the other people in rapport with the person at different levels of negotiation.

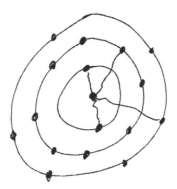

The empowerment in understanding this model of intimate rapport is that the person as the nucleus is deciding how far in another person has the right to come toward the center.

In Chemistry, an atom's first shell from the nucleus has the fewest number of electrons. Only two electrons can fill that shell or ring, which models the idea that at the deepest level of intimate rapport, the fewest people will the know the most about us. This ring is usually reserved for a spouse or a partner and perhaps a best friend, sibling or parent. This is permission to not let everybody into our most inner self, only the few we deeply desire to keep posted on our constant growth which can be subtle and profound in turns.

Then the electron rings continue to model intimate rapport negotiation, in that each ring further from the nucleus can have more and more possible electrons in orbit on them. Translating this from electrons to people means that each ring further from the nucleus contains people in rapport at more causal levels, and we meet at specific places where we match, and have a relationship there. It could be that we golf together or go to the university together for work or class, but these people will know less about us, even when what they do know is authentic and honest.

Being conscious about negotiating intimacy gives us permission to start friendships or relationships based on safety and honesty. To thrive, it is important to create relationships that are healthy in intimate rapport and reciprocal intimacy is agreed upon.

We can invite our intimate rapport with another to deepen, but we can't force and likewise we don't need to succumb to force either, if going deeper doesn't feel safe or appropriate. As an example: as work colleagues, we don't owe our personal information in the workplace. We don't purposefully hide it, we just don't share.

Our power is in knowing it is our right to decide, then giving that right to the other person also so the negotiation process is gentle and honest for both people. Knowing this information gives us the emotional freedom to connect with people more readily and create relationships that feel healthy and authentic.

CHAPTER 5

Binocular Circles with Cell Wall Biology for DNA Family vs. Spirit Family

Pattern use: to sort out the difference between feeling forced to be intimate through family ties and feeling open and supported through friendships, whether through family or not, that allow shifting of interests and lifestyles to be supported.

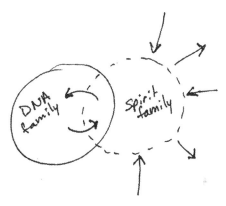

Again, these doodles are to help make a picture of a spiritual concept for growth and awareness on the journey to personal empowerment and conscious awareness. I love borrowing loosely from all of science, nature and math. This doodle is ultimately about boundaries.

People on the self-actualization and spiritual growth quest need permission to individualize the expression of who they are. Congruency and authenticity become the goal—not compliance to the family agreements.

Many of us are raised thinking that our family of origin has the right to know everything about us and our decisions even when we are adults. Other affiliations that serve as surrogate community or family, which take possession of us and make our uniqueness subservient to the group's needs, replicates the same boundary violation.

This type of family tells us if they disapprove. Without judge and jury we stand before our family, guilty of making them unhappy, while they reflect to us that we need our family to survive and must stay connected to it at all costs, even if it costs us our honesty and authenticity.

If we are going to take self-responsibility for our lives then we must give them the absolute right to decide how to respond to life, even if it is about us.

Then once they show their reaction to us, our personal power through conscious awareness can be used to decide how close or far we want to be to their reaction.

If *spiritual right action* says we must come from unconditional love and compassion, then the only question is, "How close or far can we be both emotionally and physically and still come from love?"

Only we can decide what is honest and authentic in this distance calculation, and that can be renegotiated by the second, minute, hour, day, month, or year. Sometimes the calculation we come up with will last a lifetime of a specific distance.

The calculation is made for distance both emotionally and physically. Sometimes we can be in physical proximity to a person but distant emotionally and feel peaceful and compassionate. Other times the calculation comes out that we must be distant physically but we can be emotionally available. For example: over the phone we can give support to someone emotionally but have no desire to join them in their chosen environment.

Still other times to be emotionally free and healthy we must distance ourselves both physically and emotionally to be able to hold space and feel unconditional love and compassion for a person or group of people. To be able to grow and evolve spiritually over a lifetime we must let others attend to their solitary journey as we do ours, and it can be hard when we feel like we need them—whether family or friends.

The binocular circle doodle is used to map out the awareness needed to have healthy boundaries. The two circles that overlap in the middle are the two different support systems available.

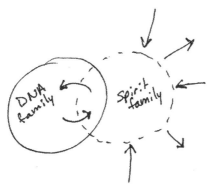

One circle represents what I call your DNA family, or family of origin. This circle represents the people you were raised with as family, and possibly extended family if they played a large role in your life; and like in my case, your family functioned in an extended way as a clan. This circle is drawn in a solid line because family of origin is set in DNA or by legal adoption, and is constant, and unchanging.

The other circle is drawn in a dotted line and slightly overlaps the family of origin circle. This dotted line represents what I call your *spirit family.*

My definition of spirit family is people who love you and support you as an authentic and honest friend. Spirit family is willing to support you while you grow and evolve through life experiences even while making mistakes, and they cheer for you in your successes. They ask nothing of you and you hold no contracts on them. They are free to come and go from that circle as they also grow and evolve because you ask nothing from them, and you expect them to grow and evolve as well.

It is understood that we don't always stay on the same page and that connection can shift like the sand over time and everyone is free to stay or free to leave as it feels right. Spirit family can have an expected subtle constant flux, and the rapport is reciprocal.

When people drift out of our spirit family circle it just means we don't match as intimately as we did before and that's OK.

Spirit family may or may not know each other in our circle. We may meet up with groups of them or they may be, in part or all, separately negotiated friendships that you have deep, intimate rapport with individually.

The spirit family circle is a permeable membrane and people come and go by osmosis so that everyone has the possibility to function in an honest openhearted way with the people that resonate.

The overlap in the middle has the solid line inside the dotted spirit family circle and the dotted line is inside the solid family of origin circle. This is the place where family of origin has the right to cross the semi-permeable membrane and enter the spirit family we have created, if they create an environment in support of growth.

I have DNA family members in my spirit family. They come in through the semi-permeable membrane, but like cell wall membranes, sometimes you have to use an active transport pump to move them back across the line when you are no longer on the same page. This process can be repeated many times with many DNA family members over an adult lifetime.

In very healthy family systems, the renegotiation of parents and siblings into adult relationships goes smoothly and the family can learn to give the same support as spirit family, which is what we are working to create for our future adults coming behind us. This can be the goal as we become empowered and healthy in our boundaries.

CHAPTER 6

Wave Pattern
for Growth and Integration

Pattern use: to lose the fear of feeling depressed when life is in a quieter phase of rest and integration. Life cannot sustain peak to peak moments without the rest period in between and it is important to respect and honor that.

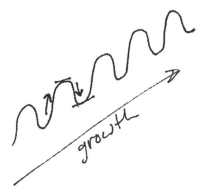

This next doodle invites us to lose fear of the rest and integration aspect of learning and growth.

In the Spiritual Doodle for the wave pattern for growth and integration, the uphill climb to the crest is bringing something to its moment of completion which implies that learning and growth is happening, and then we must go down into the trough or valley for rest and integration where the wisdom is gleaned from the experience.

The focus in our culture is on production and getting things done. We want something to show for the end of each day. Without proof of productivity the fear of being seen as lazy or not worthwhile ignites.

It is important to reconnect to the understanding that everything in our world functions on a wave or rhythm. There are sound waves, frequency, color spectrum, electricity, vibrations, radiation and heat to name some.

Nobody ever mentions that we learn in motion on a wave moving toward its crest, and then the wave balances with the rest and integration trough.

Then there is rhythm, its own kind of wave. The heart beat rhythm, the rhythm of day and night cycles, seasons in the year, each month with the moon cycle, nine month gestation of a baby, and the birthing rhythm of labor.

We are steeping in waves, vibrations, and rhythms from an atomic, cellular, organ, and body level to our rhythms of everyday life routines.

In each wave, the highest point is called the crest, and the lowest point is called the trough. I sometimes use valley to describe the lowest point.

We bring each day through to fruition then it slips into night where we rest and integrate, until we rise and meet our next day.

We bring each year of our life to a finish, and a new one rises. We also have stages that we go through in life that come to a close as the next one takes its place.

Each career or job we start will have an eventual finish, and within that career, each project and task has the same wave pattern.

We may have highlighted accomplishments during our career, but then it is time to put the metaphorical or literal trophy on the shelf and rest and integrate from our latest achievement, then move forward to the next challenge or task.

The big wave of bringing our life to fruition and then letting it go is like one big crest with the rest and integration period imagined, according to belief systems of each person.

Waves are balancing, so the higher we go up, the lower we go down. Also, the longer it takes to move to the crest the longer it may take to move through the trough or valley. We move through the troughs with grace and dignity by expecting them to be there.

A common example is college and the intensity that goes with wanting to excel at the curriculum. The excitement and stress of this high intensity experience keeps a student pushing hard until graduation.

After graduation the stress of the job search and the start of a new career feels just as intense. However, once the job is set in a routine the urgency subsides, and it's time for the rest, process, and integration time to naturally begin.

The trough with its rest, processing, and integration time will end and career life will likely start to feel normal and healthy.

When the valley of the balancing wave after a crest is expected, then it is possible to feel the effects of the valley without concern that it is pathology taking hold in the form of depression or other symptoms.

After college, I was convinced I had hypothyroidism because I felt tired, slightly depressed, and heavy, like I was dragging around. My valley after college lasted for a year.

The clues to the trough time of integration and rest is a loss of interest in external events and more retrospective and introspective thoughts and feelings. This usually happens after an achievement is accomplished or something is brought to fruition.

It is also possible during this process time to feel tired, quiet, and heavy. These are signs that the body system needs support to move through the trough instead of forcing a shift of focus away from these feelings.

It is safe to process and connect to the wisdom gained in the experience that has just come to fruition.

The next rise up the crest starts organically once the processing is finished and once again the climb to the top is underway for the next experience and learning.

There are many waves in different parts of expression at any given time. There are also waves within waves, but none of the waves seem to stick out individually.

If the wave pattern is observed over time while in a growth pattern, it will rise up. If the wave is in a destructive or negative pattern, it will still rise and fall, but it will be going in a lower direction overall.

In a lifetime most of us will spend time going in both negative and positive directions but the quest is to grow from everything while our main goal is to consciously move in a growth direction upward through time.

The desire is to be in growth overall while aware that *life functioning on a wave* needs to be surrendered to also. It is impossible to jump from crest to crest, or go from trough to trough. The work, learning, and accomplishment are in the rise to the crest. The rest, integration, and wisdom are gleaned in the trough. Balance is the key to this wave we ride for a lifetime as we evolve in experience, knowledge and wisdom.

CHAPTER 7

Acorn Pattern
for Invitation to Grow Spiritually

Pattern use: to bring assurance to a moment of extreme stress so a new perspective can be achieved and the physiology of stress can settle to aid in more creative solutions planning.

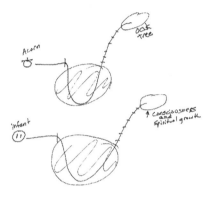

I think of this doodle as the acorn pattern. Acorns are the seeds of an oak tree and I keep a few at my desk in a bowl with rocks and other curiosities.

Acorns also look like a little head with a hat on and I have always been fascinated by how hard they are to crack open. They are the perfect little example of being a "tough nut to crack" literally, as well as how it parallels my life metaphorically.

Part of my growth is a commitment to listen and grow from intuitive whispers instead of needing heavy amounts of heat and pressure to make course corrections on my life's trajectory.

An acorn is complete to itself, and we would never say anything is missing from it, or that it looks incomplete.

An acorn also has the possible future potential as an oak tree, but doesn't have the capacity to judge itself as it remains an acorn (like the one in a bowl on my desk) and doesn't make it to a full-grown tree.

Nature models non-judgment in its silent acceptance of what is. The forest is beautiful in all of the different expressions such as trees of various species coexisting in varying forms of health, and the dead trees returning to the earth in decay on the ground.

The ground in the forest shows various forms of life and decay, as the compost of leaves and other organic material rot back into nutrients for the growing plants.

Nothing is seen as out of place to nature. Forests are seen as beautiful and nurturing to walk in and connect with.

In the Spiritual Doodle I draw an acorn and explain how the acorn is complete to itself with nothing missing from it.

We know, however, that the acorn also has a potential to become an oak tree. To become a tree an acorn must be covered with compost and earth and rot, swell, and split open before the potential of becoming that future oak tree is possible.

The point of no return is when an acorn is split open and broken. It cannot return to the acorn it once was and it hasn't even begun sending its first little shoot up to the surface of the ground. This is the point of most danger, a choice point. One choice of the acorn is to continue entropy, a movement towards chaos, until it no longer is distinguishable from the soil and compost. The acorn also has the other choice to start the growth towards its fullest expression as an oak tree.

The point of most danger is also the point of most opportunity to finally start a shoot that will eventually push out of the ground and become a seedling.

This whole process from seed to mature tree is filled with danger. All along the way something could happen to the tree that would terminate the ability to reach its highest potential.

It also takes more energy for the acorn to become an oak tree then it would to return to compost. The push to a fully mature oak tree is ongoing even in the presence of danger and possible challenge.

The next part of the doodle is a circle representing a baby with two small lines inside representing spirit/soul and physical/terminal aspects, all within the newborn child.

Then following the same trajectory as the acorn, it moves along in Time and Destiny until some form of challenge or complexity enters this person's life, likened to the acorn that was complete and now covered in earth, swelling and splitting open. A baby is complete to itself, the same as the acorn, but it doesn't have the capacity to express unconditional love and compassion. Just the seed of that potential lies in the infant.

A newborn child is a universal receiver of unconditional love and support, not yet a reflector of this type of connection. The infant needs to understand and embody what love and connection feels like while in physical body.

The baby learns this while steeping in unconditional love and support from the parents and unable to reciprocate.

A child cries out for needs of care and affection, unaware of the emotional and physical state of the sometimes exhausted parents. Then as the child grows and goes through life, it follows the path of an acorn.

An acorn also starts out small and grows to maturity and then falls from the tree to begin a life of its own away from the nurturing source of the tree. A young adult leaves home and moves through life with the knowledge and experience gained in childhood.

Nothing is missing from this young adult and he or she is complete to themselves. However, there is a higher, spiritual expression potential that is waiting for the *Law of Perfect Timing* to invite this young person to hone and polish. The facet of reflecting unconditional love and compassion is understood mainly as being the receiver in childhood and needs to be matured as a reflector to others in reciprocation, a skill grown continuously through a lifetime.

The invitation usually is delivered through a crisis or complex challenge. This is when the collapse of what used to work sends a person into grief and despair, like the acorn now swelling and splitting and dying a death of what used to be complete and knowable.

Under this heat and pressure of crisis or challenge is where the Free Will decision is made to destruct, like the composting acorn, or transform, like the little green shoot that rises out of the earth to start the transformation into a majestic tree.

Crisis and challenge can be known as heat and pressure to transform or destruct. It is the most dangerous time and the time of most potential to journey into the higher expression possible in a human.

The human, as a spirit in a physical body, has the possibility to come from love and compassion from Free Will instead of reflexively using survival strategies only. Spiritual growth, in my definition, is to be able to come from love and compassion—first for ourselves, then for others—under deeper and deeper pressure as we grow.

Crisis is where we examine our willingness to embark on a spiritual journey that will last a lifetime of growth, as static perfection is not a goal nor required for joy, peace and happiness.

If the decision is made to destruct under this heat and pressure, then that will be lived out as your reality based on circumstances.

Nobody can talk an individual out of that choice because Free Will is set up so that either choice is truth. Only the intention to see it one way or another directs which expression of truth is unfolding.

When the decision is made to transform or grow spiritually from the crisis, or invitation from the Law of Perfect Timing, it takes more energy to create order from the chaos.

Initially it is harder to grow from complexities and challenges, and entropy into continued chaos will seem easier.

However, as the downward spiral of despair and destruction continues toward entropy, at any time a person can decide to start to grow instead of destruct.

Who can judge what it will take to give a person, or ourselves, enough heat and pressure to do the splitting open to start the tender green shoot of new spiritual awareness? The Law of Non-Judgment allows love and support from others to continue, without agenda, so the Free Will decision, empowerment, and wisdom belong to the person in crisis and challenge.

Unlike an acorn, a person is put into the heat and pressure of complex challenges more than once. Each time it is possible to come out with yet a more refined spiritual awareness, if we choose to grow this awareness through Free Will.

The ability to understand love and compassion is only from the spiritual system within each individual.

Intellectually it is never going to make sense to choose to love or have compassion. Intellectually it only makes our life more at risk to suffer and be hurt. To the terminal aspect of self, which is all that dies someday, the most important aspect of life is survival.

The Spiritual aspect of self understands that it is of little importance to be in or out of physical body, and is immortal; it only seeks to grow the ability to share love and reflect the energy of what is bigger than us.

We are here to be a reflection of the energy called love that everything emanates from. Unlike trees, rocks, water, animals, and plants that express *spiritual right action* wordlessly in fractals of perfection and acceptance of what is, with true non-judgment and humbleness, we have Free Will and the ability to reflect on our life and choose how to respond, whether consciously or unconsciously from fear or love.

As each person reflects love as the result of growth through challenges, it's easier for others to share this template for growth.

Modeling is the most powerful way to teach spiritual truth, whereas evangelizing is a form of violence, because it shares information and opinions with those who did not ask and Free Will is not being respected.

Modeling teaches without words but is willing to answer any question in an openhearted, honest way, only as the truth as we understand it at this time. Modeling does not mind if the person asking embodies any of the information at that time or ever, and love and respect for the person asking is reflected through the embodiment of love and respect of self through the Law of Equal Value.

The Law of Equal Value allows each person to be where ever they are at on their solitary journey towards awareness and reciprocal sharing of love.

This Spiritual Doodle maps out growth potential through the complex challenges of our lives for the benefit of better understanding unconditional love and compassion for ourselves and others, so we can share love in reciprocal rapport as each of us will take our turn being invited to grow.

Modeling our growth is the most loving way to serve another, and it first serves us for our own joy, peace and happiness.

CHAPTER 8

Binary System of Fear versus Love

Pattern use: to return an individual to self-responsibility regarding how they choose to respond to life during times of high stress or complexity.

Binary

Fear	Love
−	+
NO	yes
Black	white
Partical	wave
Sympathetic	parasympathetic
0	1
not for me	for me

Fear versus Love has already been discussed as the binary system of free choice in previous chapters. I often draw it out separately to explain the power of choice.

When results in life are incompatible with desired results, understanding Free Will is where you have the power to create change.

Free Will, as discussed with Time and Destiny, is the place where you have the power to recreate your life and work with the *potentials in the future* for new outcomes.

We also must become aware that reflexive responding in patterns gets us the same results in variations while the pattern drives itself.

Awareness of patterns driving is what returns us to choice, along with understanding how Free Will operates as a filter system that determines how each choice is made. A return to self-responsibility is made possible through this empowered awareness.

Binary

Fear	Love
−	+
NO	yes
Black	white
Partical	wave
Sympathetic	parasympathetic
0	1
Not for me	for me

The doodle is drawn with a vertical line and a short horizontal line toward the top. Fear is on one side, and love is on the other written above the horizontal line. Underneath the horizontal line I write all the repeating patterns of the binary system that parallel Free Will, and functions to anchor understanding.

Our computers use zero and one at the most basic level of function. Quanta, in physics, function as either a particle or a wave.

Our nervous system has the parasympathetic system for peacetime functions such as digestion, balancing hormones, and repairing tissues, and the sympathetic nervous system for fight or flight. These two nervous systems function on an inverse sliding scale of each other, when one is more active the other is less active.

Then there is Black, which absorbs all color, and White, which reflects all color. Plus and minus, or positive and negative are the polar opposites in binary system.

The two basic answers we give each moment are either: yes or no; or this is for me or not for me. We navigate life in this binary system of—this works for me and this doesn't work for me.

I liken coming from fear as alternating current because it is: I win, you lose; or I lose, you win. In this fear based model of existence, both winning and losing are experienced and much can be learned from both sides.

The other side of the binary system is love, and this is like the *direct current model* which functions in I win, you win, and the greater whole has more potential to win.

The experience of *spiritual right action* can give us more courage to be conscious enough to come from this model, and it drives from peace, love, and compassion.

We will spend our lives alternating between fear and love. We can learn valuable information choosing from love or fear if we suspend judgment and use discernment to glean wisdom and understanding from the result we acquire.

The learning is set up so we recognize when we have come from fear, or are about to, and return to love, first because it serves us, then others, and the greater whole for good.

Reconciling Free Will is the key to world peace and individual empowerment because it allows self-responsibility for choices, actions and outcomes.

We are hard-wired to want to live in peace with love and compassion, but it takes courage to go first so that peace and love can be modeled as the most powerful way to spread the potential.

CHAPTER 9

Concentric Rings of Belonging

Pattern use: to remind a person of their connection to all of humanity starting at the most intimate connection to self, then family then all the way to a global community. It is each individual's decision where the rings become walls that keep out connection and form division and isolation.

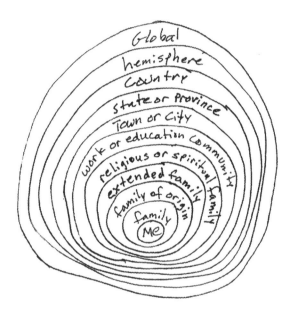

When a pebble is thrown into a pond of flat, still water, there is a small circle where the pebble entered the water. Then small rings spread out from that initial spot and grow larger and larger with more rings following the first out from the center. This is the visual for the *concentric rings of belonging* doodle.

The center represents you. As the rings move out they represent other ways that you are included in a group moving out in levels of connection from most intimate to global.

After the center represents you, the next ring may be your spouse and children, if you have them. Your family of origin is in the next ring. As you move away from the center there can be your extended family, including your spouse's family.

Then the rings start into community such as your religious or spiritual community, education community, work community, town, village, or city, state, province, region, hemisphere, and finally your global connection to all of humanity through shared humanness, perhaps the most casual connection but still they're influencing who we know we are as an individual.

The concentric rings of belonging helps us take an interesting look at how we connect. However, at which ring do they become walls that divide us?

Everyone has these rings around them, and we each decide which ring is the first ring of dividing, and usually from there to the outside of the rings will be a wall, not connection.

At first glance that looks like the safe way to live and perhaps for survival it works well, just like personal body armor that is literal or metaphorical.

If our goal, however, is to thrive then it will be important to expand our rings of connection, with our growth, so that eventually our goal is feeling that the whole world is our neighborhood and we have love and compassion for all.

We get to decide on our readiness to grow and evolve to include all of humanity as equal value to ourselves. Growth is organic and personal and we must live in the paradox of having nothing but time while living in a mortal body.

Growth is our only goal, and it first serves us to feel the joy of honest openhearted rapport in a growing circle of connection. Then through modeling, it invites others to find courage to come from love and openhearted sharing, which then serves in one small way for the potential for world peace. We are all accountable to adding to the potential for world peace, (the ability to sustain love and compassion for all— including ourselves) as the highest calling each of us has while here in body.

CHAPTER 10

Equation for Trust and Love

Pattern use: to assure a person that it's fine to restore trust over time it doesn't need to be automatic.

$$\frac{experience}{time} = trust$$

$$trust + commitment = Love$$

This doodle is a small and simple sketch of the nuts and bolts to intimate rapport for people in relationships. I use it to show the mechanics that drive trust and love.

The equation for trust is experience over time equals trust.

I write out trust plus commitment equals love in the form of a math problem.

I have spoken to so many people who want to love people they can't trust. They need the equation to see that there is an irrational aspect to what they want if trust is absent.

When a person has been betrayed it is important to see that only experience over time will really allow trust to grow organically again. It is fair to say people can change and grow. That is the premise this whole book is based on. Experience over time will allow a person healing their life to model that the growth is allowing trust to be reignited.

Trust and commitment are needed for love to flourish. It is impossible to feel safe and supported if the commitment is fragile or trust is absent.

This doodle helps a person come to terms with what may not be working in a relationship. Then the individual can process the choice of inviting the person to work towards repairing the connection to intimate rapport, or disbanding from it as the best way to return to unconditional love and compassion for the other person and themselves.

It is important to realize you can only *invite* another person to choose to grow; it is not possible to force. This awareness is the Law of Humbleness and we can only be responsible for the modeling of our truth.

In any relationship that is challenged, it is best to make decisions on whether to stay or disband from how best to love ourselves and the other person.

CHAPTER 11

Inverse Scale of Consciousness

Pattern use: to explain the responsibility to respond to others from peace and love that is inherent with the desire to live consciously.

As a person gains consciousness and the power that goes with awareness, it is possible to use it for peace or for harm. There is a governor on consciousness that is built on an inverse sliding scale, similar to the parasympathetic nervous system regulating peacetime function and sympathetic nervous system regulating fight or flight.

The governor for conscious awareness works in a self-regulating way. Through free choice we get to decide if we use awareness to harm another or ourselves, but the response to the *growth in consciousness* is to lower our awareness as not to see the violence we are committing.

The more consciousness is grown, the more awareness grows of what entails subtle acts of violence. The more violence is chosen, then the more shutdown of awareness is needed to not have to reconcile our violent acts.

We may all agree that hurting another person is wrong, but with awareness we start to see more subtle acts of violation. If growth of consciousness is our goal, then those acts must be omitted from our choices so we can sit peacefully with our awareness. This is the more demanding path; it is easy to understand why not all embrace consciousness. Intuitively, the high demand of self-accountability necessary is understood.

It is an easy slide into acting out in anger through committing violence. It takes much more energy and creativity to channel the emotion of anger into a conscious decision to change what is no longer working in the environment for the betterment of all, including self. Anger is just being used as one example that comes up often.

Growth in awareness which is consciousness, comes wired to the willingness to become less and less violent. It becomes clear what growth and consciousness means as we evolve. That is why conscious people are powerful and self-governing. It is the inside out model of power that is willing to do the right thing even if nobody is watching, because they refuse to violate themselves. It is the price you pay for becoming aware.

Example Doodle Session

I have been a dental hygienist for 26 years at this writing. I have used pieces of tray paper for scribbling notes of special instructions for patients' oral care. I rip this tray paper into the size of the note and give it to them. It has a unique feeling of being for them only and those quick scribbles are well received.

I do the same thing with the mapping out of the patterns for Spiritual Doodle. I draw on yellow lined paper that I buy in bulk. I keep all my drawings on one side as I talk about these concepts and draw them out. Then I will rip off the paper and give it to my client to anchor the discussion and let them reflect on their new awareness as applied to their personal story.

In my mind, body, spirit integration work, I may only draw one pattern. I will usually just draw the pattern up in the rolled over page of the tablet or in the margins. It helps to see the drawing to anchor the awareness.

This system of Spiritual Doodle is easy to do, but profound in its facilitation. Awareness and re-engagement of inner courage and curiosity is the goal, so an empowered person can go and learn in the rich matrix of life, where chaos makes everything possible, and creates the ability to learn and grow wisdom possible and interesting.

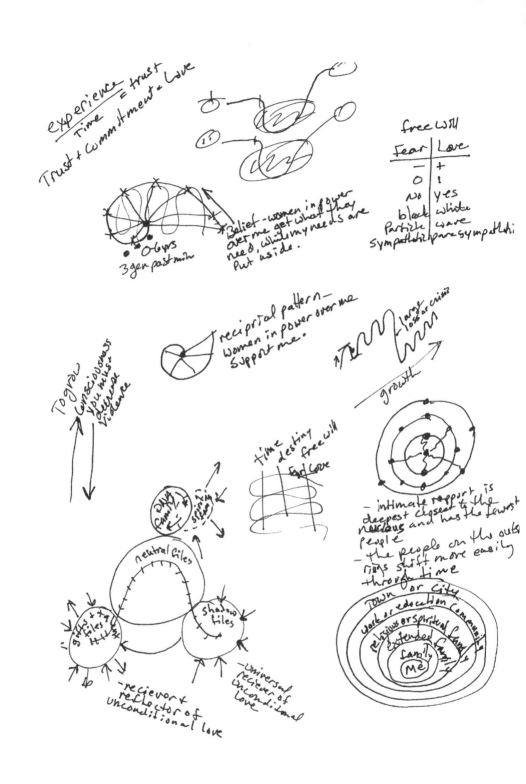

Final Thoughts

I invite you to not over think your drawings of these doodles. It's that they are infused with your knowledge and wisdom that matters most.

Let it be easy. Let it be spontaneous, organic, meaningful, messy, eclectic and fun.

Reading List

Here is a partial list of books that have helped me see into life deeper and make wiser more conscious choices in how to proceed and engage in a life journey worth taking. I am grateful to all authors that have been willing to share their knowledge with me through their books.

Bartlett, Richard, D.C., H.D. (2010). *The Physics of Miracles, Tapping Into the Field of Consciousness Potential*

Braden, Gregg (2009). *Fractal Time*

Despenza, Dr. Joe (2015). *You Are the Placebo: Making Your Mind Matter*

Faber, Adele and Mazlish, Elaine (1990). *Liberated Parents, Liberated Children: Your Guide to a Happier Family*

Lerner, Harriet, Ph.D. (1989). *The Dance of Intimacy: A Women's Guide to Courageous Acts of Change in Key Relationships*

Lipton, Bruce H. Ph.D. (2005). *The Biology of Belief*

Littauer, Florence (1986). *Your Personality Tree*

Mate, Gabor, M.D. (2003). *When the Body Says No: The Cost of Hidden Stress*

Northrup, Christine, M.D. (1998). *Women's Bodies, Women's Wisdom: Creating Physical and Emotional Health and Healing*

Ornish, Dean, M.D. (1998). *Love & Survival, the Scientific Basis for the Healing Power of Intimacy*

Schulz, Mona Lisa, M.D., Ph.D. (1998). *Awakening Intuition: Using Your Mind-Body Network for Insight*

Printed in the United States
By Bookmasters